Tools for Emotional Well-Being

Ask for help

Breathe

Count to 10

Detach and describe (I feel ...)

Express gratitude

Forgive

Grin from within

Hang with friends and family

Invite ideas

Joke

Know yourself

Laugh

Meditate

Nap

Observe

Play

Quiet and calm

Release

Sing or hum

Tap or twitch

Use your words

Visualize a solution

Walk your talk

eXercise

Yield

Zoom in to get a clearer picture

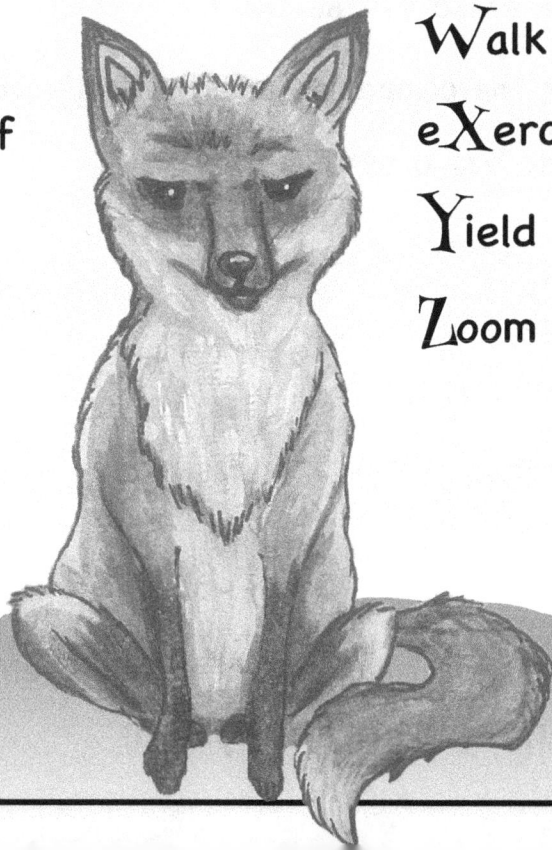

Published © 2019 by Serendipitous Entertainment
Text © 2019 by Sarahndipity Johnsen
Illustrations © 2019 by Amanda Dumont and Serendipitous Entertainment
Design by Heidi Bassignani
Edited by Mary Greene

ISBN: 978-0-999366-1-4-1

For further support, look for the companion book, *Animals Get Emotional.*

ISBN: 978-0-999366-3-4

SERENDIPITOUS ENTERTAINMENT
PO Box 23366
Glade Park, CO 81523

Learn about other books, music, curriculum, videos, live events, and more!
www.AnimalsGetFunky.com

Color Your Emotions

Dealing with Big Feelings

Serendipitous
ENTERTAINMENT

SERENDIPITOUS ENTERTAINMENT

Affectionate Angelfish

Affectionate Angelfish treat each other with kindness.
Around close friends and family, they feel blessed.

Bored Boar

If you are feeling bored, look around
and realize life is your playground.

Confused Camel

When you're feeling bewildered or perplexed,
find one piece of the puzzle then the next.

Depressed Dolphin

Let someone know if you are lonely or have lost your flow.
Together, it's easier to process and let go.

Excited Elk

When you are tuned in to an excited thought or notion,
Get going. Put this emotion into motion.

Frustrated Fox

When you feel it's not okay to lose,
see the other side because you get to choose.

Guilty Gecko

If you're feeling low like Guilty Gecko,
then find your words and let an apology flow.

Happy Hedgehogs

Be content with this moment right now.
Let go of past and future, just allow.

Infatuated Indri

You'll feel strongly about many people you know.
With some you'll feel off, and with others you'll feel aglow.

Jealous Jackal

Celebrate success to calm stress and tension.
Look for positive ways to gain attention.

Kindhearted Killer Whale

Be compassionate, thoughtful, and sweet.
Charity, and one for all, can't be beat.

Loving Lizards

How can you bring unity to your community
and embrace life with generosity?

Melancholy Moose

When you are feeling sad, tell someone close.
Turn that frown around, and light up the shadows.

Neglected Nile Crocodile

When others' thoughts are busy and can't be on you,
be your own best friend. There are many fun things to do.

Optimistic Ostrich

When you dream BIG, hope, and keep looking up,
the brighter side of life usually shows up.

Pessimistic Platypus

If you expect misfortune, your thoughts often make it true.
Turn it around, shift your view, and let possibilities shine through.

Quiet Quoll

Collecting thoughts is much easier in silence.
Through meditation, you can find balance.

Relieved Rattlesnake

When Fear creeps into your brain,
shake off the tension or strain.

Surprised Seal

When things happen without warning, it may feel like a quick shift.
Feelings of wonder and astonishment can be a gift.

Tired Tiger

If you are feeling worn out, it's time rest and unwind.
Sleep and relaxation are essential bear in mind.

Unhappy Urchin

Take deep breaths for anger, a nap when you're tired,
or grab a snack with a friend that you've admired.

Violent Vervet Monkey

There are many unsafe ways to play.
Use your words, not the Violent Vervet Monkey way.

Worried Walrus

Count your blessings, and let gratitude shine through.
You are safe and sound, not living in a zoo.

XOXO Xixiasaurus

XOXO, kisses and hugs, are for those who treat you right.
This feeling of unconditional love makes your heart take flight.

Yearning Yellow Baboon

When a feeling of longing comes on strong,
you can count, tap or tickle, or sing a silly song.

Zany Zebu

Be a kid! Let your hair flow wild, loose, and free.
Be brave. Shine your light for the world to see.

Music, Books, Curriculum, Videos, Puppetry, Games, and More!

Sign up for the Animals Get Funky experience and you'll gain access to exclusive opportunities, FREE downloads, videos, VIP virtual events, and other funky fun.

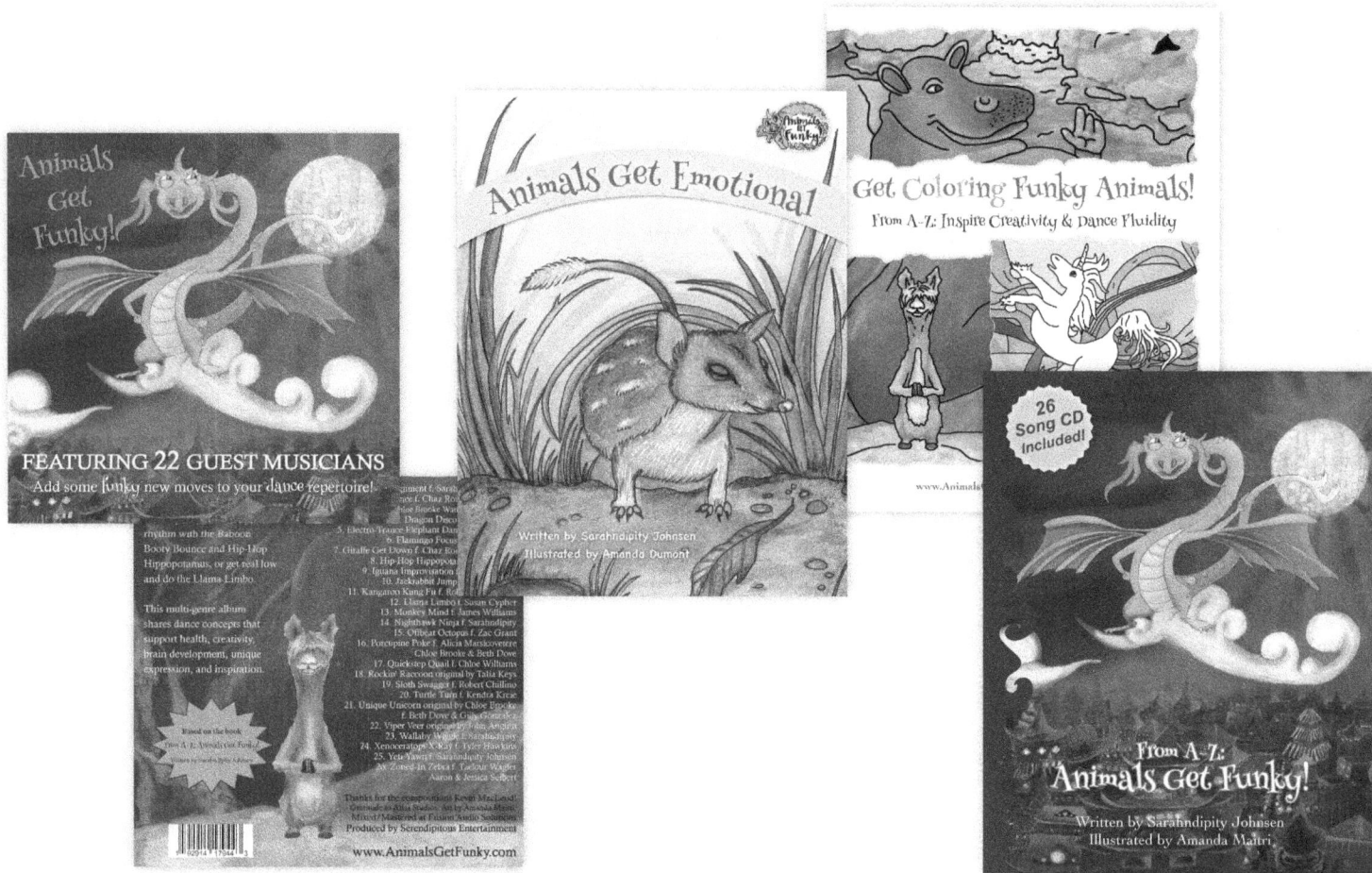

www.AnimalsGetFunky.com

Are you an educator or homeschool facilitator?
Connect & sign up for FREE activities for your classroom!

Subscribe to our YouTube channel to see BONUS FEATURES of these wild friends in action!

Like, listen, follow, download, purchase, and stream! We make it easy.